EXTREME SPORTS AND STUNTS™

EXTREME MOVIE STUNTS

Don Rauf

rosen publishing's rosen central
New York

Published in 2020 by The Rosen Publishing Group, Inc.
29 East 21st Street, New York, NY 10010

First Edition

Library of Congress Cataloging-in-Publication Data

Names: Rauf, Don, author.
Title: Extreme movie stunts / Don Rauf.
Description: First edition. | New York : Rosen Publishing, 2020. | Series: Extreme sports and stunts | Includes bibliographical references and index.
Identifiers: LCCN 2019009434| ISBN 9781725347373 (library bound) |
ISBN 9781725347366 (pbk.)
Subjects: LCSH: Stunt performers—Juvenile literature.
Classification: LCC PN1995.9.S7 R38 2020 | DDC 791.402/8—dc23
LC record available at https://lccn.loc.gov/2019009434

Manufactured in the United States of America

Disclaimer: Do not attempt any of the stunts in this book.

CONTENTS

INTRODUCTION

In the climactic scene in the movie *Wonder Woman* (2017), the superhero defeats the villain Ludendorff in a spectacular fight that ends with a slow-motion kick, sending Ludendorff crashing through a window. While it looks like the lead actress, Gal Gadot, is delivering the thrashing, much of the action was actually performed by her stunt double, Caitlin Dechelle. In interviews, Dechelle said that one of her favorite stunts in that movie was the high kick to Ludendorff that sent him flying from the tower. Though movie and television stars get all the attention, stunt performers like Dechelle make all the action possible. They jump from speeding cars, dive off cliffs, and take all the hits.

Developing a diverse set of physical skills pays off in this field because stunt work requires such a wide range of strong athletic abilities. A film may call for wall climbing, skiing, scuba diving, skateboarding, skydiving, martial arts, or wrestling. Stunt work poses more danger than most sports. And while they take steps to keep themselves safe, these professionals can suffer injuries, some of which can be very serious. But the job is rewarding because it allows you to be both physical and creative.

This resource will hurtle you into the death-defying world of stunt performing. You'll get a glimpse at the various standard action sequences—how they are planned, rehearsed, and executed. The chapters cover safety measures and gear used behind the scenes and

Stunt performers fly through the air on the set of the movie *Sherlock Holmes: A Game of Shadows* (2011). The job is dangerous, so performers always wear safety gear, usually hidden under their clothing.

explain how you can seek out professional training if you think working in stunt performance may be for you.

Top Hollywood stunt double Danielle Burgio says the key ingredient to this work is is a love for it: "It's easy to master a skill when you're passionate about it."

CHAPTER ONE

DELIVERING SPILLS AND THRILLS

Performing stunts for film and television goes back to the early days of the motion picture industry. Silent movies—especially slapstick comedies—featured many gutsy action scenes in which the actors put themselves in perilous situations without any serious safety precautions. Silent-era comedian Buster Keaton, who was famous for his elaborate physical gags, called safety equipment "coward's paraphernalia." In a nail-biting scene from his film *Steamboat Bill, Jr.*, Keaton stands dazed in front of a house after a cyclone. When the two-ton house front falls over, he is positioned so the window of the house passes over him as it comes crashing to the ground. Keaton had only inches of clearance on all sides. If he stood just a little bit off, the wall would have crushed him.

Spend some time with the classic old silent films and you'll see Harold Lloyd dangling from the minute hand on a tower clock in *Safety Last* and Charlie Chaplin roller-skating blindfolded to the edge of a ledge in *Modern Times.* After serving as a pilot in World War I, Earl Burgess performed harrowing stunts in silent movies—jumping from plane to

Stunt performance dates back to the early silent movie days. Slapstick comedies, such as *Safety Last* with Harold Lloyd (1923), featured death-defying "gags."

plane and leaping from an aircraft to a speeding train. Unfortunately, while filming one fight scene on the wings, he fell to his death. He refused to ever use a parachute.

RISKY BUSINESS

In the world of stunt performing, these dangerous acts are still called gags—even if they aren't always funny. As film and television became more popular and technologically advanced, the audiences still craved the exploits of the stunt performers to bring action to the screen.

Over time, stunt performers have taken more and more safety measures to prevent injuries. The Center for Safety in the Arts reported forty stunt-related deaths in the movie and television industries from 1980 to 1990. From 2002 through 2016, no stunt workers died from their work. However, in 2017, a stuntman on *The Walking Dead* television series died after falling 22 feet (6.7 meters) to the pavement and a stuntwoman in *Deadpool 2* died in a motorcycle accident on set. The motto for stunt coordinators, performers, and directors today is: safety first!

In the film world today, some stunt workers have worried that computer-generated imagery (CGI) would put them out of work. Why not save on money and possible bodily harm by producing all action sequences using software and special effects? The fact is that action sequences created solely with computer technology do not look as real. Andy Armstrong, a stunt coordinator for *The Amazing Spider-Man* (2012), said in an interview in *The Guardian*, "When CGI first came about, stunt people thought 'that's the end of our business, everyone's going to be replaced by computers.' That hasn't happened, because there's still a certain authenticity to seeing a real human do something."

A PLAN OF ACTION

To help ensure that no one gets hurt, stunts are planned carefully. The stunt performer, stunt coordinator, and director discuss and map out exactly how a stunt will be done. Many filmmakers storyboard their stunt scenes, which is sketching out the action, shot by shot, with a series of images. The storyboard looks a lot like a comic book and is a blueprint to choreograph the scene. Some directors will take the images and animate them with dialog and music in place. These are called animatics, and they give directors a better idea of how the final result should come out. A stunt coordinator will determine the risks involved and how to protect the performer. He or she will also figure out what equipment might be needed.

Before shooting begins, the stunt person may rehearse the action several times. Rehearsal helps ensure that everything will go as planned when it comes time to shoot. This may require walking through the action step by step and identifying exactly where and when each part of the action takes place. John Badham, director of *Saturday*

Night Fever (1977), *Dracula* (1979), and *WarGames* (1983), among other films, has said that he must understand exactly what the stunt person will do and that it matches what he asked for.

Sometimes a cameraperson has to be almost as fearless and athletic as the stunt performer. In *The Bourne Ultimatum* (2007), Matt Damon leaps from a rooftop over an alley and into an open window of another building. In the movie, the

To film dangerous stunts, the director will use storyboards of the action and review them with the actor, just as director Brian De Palma is doing here with Tom Cruise.

camera closely follows Damon as he makes the jump. To capture that action, the cameraman had to jump along with the actor. To do that, the film crew put him in a harness connected to a cord that allowed him to jump off the roof behind Damon and then safely dangle after completing the shot.

GETTING BLOWN UP IS ALL IN A DAY'S WORK

Days on set can be very long, running up to fourteen hours or more. Often, the director will want to do a few takes as well to make sure he or she has filmed the scene. Sometimes, retakes are impossible because something expensive has to be destroyed. A director may not have a budget to flip a car twice or blow up a yacht more than once.

Doing it right the first time was key for a scene that stunt person Mike Owen performed in *The Punisher* (2004), a movie based on a Marvel Comics superhero. In one scene that is just a minute on screen, the hero gets blasted off a dock when gas canisters explode. Owen prepared for a week. The crew set up a large hoist and cable. The wire would attach to Owen and when the explosion went off, the wire would yank him, sending him flying in the air and into the water.

He prepared for days testing the speed and altitude of the stunt. The wire would be erased later in postproduction. The film crew had rigged up a special flare that would send a fireball at Owen. As the fireball grew, the wire had to jerk Owen off the dock with split-second timing.

Getting thrown from a motorcycle while on fire is just part of the job of a stunt person. Fire-protective clothing and gel protects against burns and crew stand by in case of a medical emergency.

To protect himself from the heat, Owen wore special Nomex underwear (garments that firefighters wear). The underwear had been soaking in icy water for extra protection. He also slathered his face and hair with a special gel that stunt workers use to protect themselves from burns.

On the day of the shoot, six cameras were focused on Owen. As the fireball rushed toward Owen's face, the wire yanked him off the dock, propelled him high in the air, and splashed him down into the water. Divers were at the ready to scoop him up and bring him to dry land. When Owen surfaced, he gave a thumb's up and the crew applauded. Getting blown up by a fireball is just part of an average day for a stunt performer.

WHY WORK WITH STUNT PERFORMERS?

Actor Tom Cruise likes to perform many of his own stunts. But when leaping from one building to another while filming *Mission: Impossible—Fallout* (2018), the superstar broke his ankle, even though he had been rigged up with a wire to soften the impact. The injury put him out of action for six weeks. If the accident had been worse, it could have stopped the entire project. If a movie star gets severely injured while filming, a production can lose millions of dollars that it has invested. This is one of the major reasons why the film and television industry uses stunt doubles. Actors also need to use their energy and time to simply learn their lines and act. A stunt may have to be filmed several times before they get it right and that can take a lot of stamina.

THE RIGHT PERSON FOR THE JOB

The key to using a stunt double is to make sure the transition in the film is seamless. The audience has to believe that the double is the actor when watching the movie. Marguerite Derricks, who cast Emma Stone's double for the movie *Crazy, Stupid, Love* (2011), said in an interview in *Dance Spirit*, "You have to match them up, especially the body type, height and skin tone—you even need similar facial features for side shots."

A stunt person can modify some physical features (like hair color) and wear matching wardrobe, but precise measurements of height and weight are a must on a stunt person's résumé. Sometimes a director will have to find more than one stunt person to complete all the action scenes. Jennifer Beals's movements in the movie *Flashdance* (1983) required three doubles—a French dancer, a break dancer, and a gymnast.

A stunt person has to be a bit of an actor as well. Stuntman Vic Armstrong wrote in his autobiography, *The Adventures of the World's Greatest Stuntman*, that he carefully studied how actor Christopher Reeves moved so he could better mimic him in the movie *Superman* (1978). "How does the character move? How does he punch? … So if I was performing a stunt as say, Superman, I had to be that character with the same mannerisms as the actor playing him. I couldn't just do my own thing, because that's when a stunt looks like a stunt and stands out like a sore thumb."

In a scene for *Nightmare on Elm Street* (1984), the character Freddy Kruger gets set on fire and charges up some stairs. The director felt that the stuntman didn't move like the lead actor, so he filmed the scene again—this time setting the lead actor ablaze. Stunt performers will often work closely with the lead actors to help them perform as much of a stunt as possible. If the actor can perform part of a fight, it will look more authentic when the double takes over and the scene is edited to come together as one fight.

CHAPTER TWO

ACTION GEAR REQUIRED

Without the right equipment, many stunt people would wind up injured or even in the hospital. As stunt performing has become more of an art and awareness of safety has grown, professionals have designed specific gear to carry out the stunts and protect these risk takers.

ABSORBING THE BLOWS

Padding is a simple but essential form of protection that helps these professionals from getting too banged up. For a fight scene where a performer may be repeatedly punched, kicked, and thrown around, padding underneath the clothes can help prevent bruising.

The stunt actors who own and operate the stunt equipment facility the Action Factory, in Los Angeles, California, design and sell padding that is streamlined so it looks natural under clothing but still absorbs the force of impact. Body pads are designed to protect knees, elbows, chest, and back. Padded shorts, created to wear beneath pants, protect the tailbone and hips.

To keep bruises and more serious injuries to a minimum, stunt performers rely on a wide range of padding and fire-resistant gear.

Many stunt performers also wear compression garments, such as snugly fitting t-shirts, shorts, socks, and underwear. Usually made from the stretchy fabric spandex, compression clothes can help prevent injuries, reduce muscle strain, wick away sweat, and improve performance.

Sometimes, stunt performers wear more protective body armor, which can be made from a material called thermoplastic Kevlar, which is bulletproof. Body armor may be rigged with small explosive devices called squibs. When these are remotely detonated, packets of corn syrup mixed with red food coloring erupt, looking like bullet wounds.

Protective cushioning is used to break all sorts of falls in stunt work. The stunt double for actor Jim Caviezel lands on a mat during filming of the television show *Person of Interest*.

Often stuntwomen may be wearing skirts or dresses that expose their legs, making it difficult to wear any padding that will go unnoticed. One time, stuntwoman Vera Lam had to take a fall wearing only a towel. Stuntwoman Tammie Baird discovered that she could protect her exposed skin by wearing gel pads that were soaked in tea to match her skin tone. The stunt crew on the film *Suicide Squad* (2016) figured out a way to create a harness that would fit underneath the microshorts worn by actress Margot Robbie who played the villain Harley Quinn.

SOFT LANDINGS FOR HARD FALLS

In addition to cushioning their bodies, stunt performers are safeguarded by different types of mats, crash pads, and air bags. For lesser falls, a crash pad made of polyurethane foam may be placed on the ground to cushion a body. When performers plummet from great heights, the inflatable air bag is typically set up to break their falls. Developed in the 1970s, the airbag replaced the use of stacked-up cardboard boxes. With the right airbag, a person can fall off a building that is twenty stories high. The airbags themselves can be massive, sometimes measuring more than 20 feet (6.7 m) high and weighing 1 ton (.9 metric ton).

For even greater dives, a daredevil may use an elasticized bungee cord. A long bungee made it possible for stuntman Wayne Michaels to plunge 720 feet (219 m) off the Contra Dam in Switzerland at the beginning of the James Bond film *Golden Eye* (1995). Michaels fainted at the end of his spectacular plunge.

BLOW BY BLOW: CHOREOGRAPHING A FIGHT SCENE

Spectacular fight scenes in film and television take days of planning and rehearsal. An improvised fight scene will not look good. The more precise the movements in a fight are, the better. The sequence of the action is often staged to be irregular. A scene that just shows hit after hit becomes boring. But if the sequence is a hit to face, a kick, swing, and a miss, the varied action makes it more interesting for the viewer.

Performers have to be aware of their footwork and not to crowd each other. Even as they focus on the choreography of a fight, the stunt performers must remember that they are acting a role and should think about the character and story motivation.

The first step is writing down the actual series of actions to be performed and drawing the key actions in some sort of storyboard. If the stunt people can visualize how the final scene should look, it helps them bring the director's vision to life. Just as in a stage play, the fight coordinator will block the scene with the actors—precisely positioning them as they move through their actions. The performers also have to know the exact set. Are they on the deck of a boat or in a back alley or an office? And what props are involved—bottles, umbrellas, tables, garbage can lids, etc.? All the preparation is often called previs, short for previsualization.

When it comes time to shoot the scene, the performers keep up their stamina and duplicate their moves for each take, often so cameras can capture the fight from different angles.

TAKING FLIGHT

Getting actors airborne can require harnesses, wiring, bungees, winches, trampolines, springboards, and other specialized equipment. To really fly through the air, an actor may wear a harness attached to a wire. A lifting device called a winch may be used to raise the person connected to the line. In filmmaking today, the winch can be programmed with a computer so the pattern of the winch's movements can be repeated precisely in filming various takes.

Connected to wires, which are later edited out, the stunt double in *The Amazing Spider-Man* appears to sail through the air.

Sometimes, a stunt coordinator sets up an air ram to propel a person through the air. The air ram is basically a catapult. When an individual steps on it, a sensor triggers the device to release and spring forward, sending that person sailing high in the air. It's often used to simulate the effects of an explosion.

HANDLING PROP WEAPONS

Many action scenes require skilled handling of prop weapons, such as guns, knives, and swords. Actors may need to hold a firearm in the same manner as a federal agent would or fire submachine guns. The guns fire blank cartridges but they still produce a loud bang and muzzle flash that can take some getting used to.

If they simulate a knife fight, performers learn to carefully handle a blade and simulate hand-to-hand combat without injuring anyone. A stunt person may even do battle with a chainsaw, using a modified version with a rubber chain to avoid serious injuries. Other movie weapons may include nunchakus, lances, clubs, maces, bayonets, and bows and arrows.

CHAPTER THREE

TRAINING TO DEFY DEATH ... SAFELY

A stunt person's main instrument is his or her body, and keeping it in top shape requires many, many hours of training and exercise each week. In an interview in *Men's Health*, Damien Walters says that his goal is to be as light but strong as possible. He does intensive calisthenics and movement exercises. He often puts on weights and jumps, to train himself to jump as high as possible. The stuntman portraying Chris Hemsworth's character Thor in the *Avengers* movies prepared with two workouts per day, five to six days a week for three months. The routine included sprinting on the treadmill, chin-ups, dips, push-ups, and weight lifting to build up his arms and shoulders to match those of the mighty Thor.

REVVING UP THE BODY

Most stunt people were athletic as kids and before entering the world of stunt performance—some are gymnasts or martial arts experts or avid mountain climbers or acrobats. Parkour and freerunning also can both provide terrific preparation because they involve getting through a series of obstacles by running, climbing, swinging, and jumping. (Freerunning only differs from parkour in that it incorporates elaborate flips and stylish acrobatic moves.) Cheerleading can provide great training for stunt work as well because it requires teamwork, stamina, flexibility, and sometimes flipping and flying through the air. Students of stunt performance often build on these experiences to become stunt performers.

In her book *The Stuntwoman's Workout*, stunt double Danielle Burgio says that she knew from an early age that she loved athletics and performing. At age eleven, she began to study dance and made that her career into young adulthood. When she auditioned and landed her first role in John Carpenter's 1998 film *Vampires*, she discovered that the body mechanics, flexibility, and choreography of dance training all applied to stunt performing.

After her first filming experience, Burgio had countless bruises but was ecstatic. She had found the career for her. She went on to perform many stunts in movies and television, perhaps most notably the *Matrix* series and *The Walking Dead*.

Because actors come in all shapes and sizes, stunt performers of all different dimensions are needed as well. Burgio encourages all types of people who are physically fit and interested in this field to pursue it. They can be of any body type but they have to be fit. She advises budding stunt people to be active every day and push themselves. Knowing the human body well and how it operates can help.

As a regular Hollywood stunt performer, Danielle Burgio wrote *The Stuntwoman's Workout*, which provides exercises and dieting advice to keep the body in top condition for stunt work.

MAKING MUSCLES

Building strength is important because so many stunts require muscle power, and strength helps prevent injuries. Many stunt workers increase their brawn through weight lifting. Generally, less repetitions, or reps, with heavier weights add size while more reps with lighter weights tone the body. The main rule is to exercise until you have muscle "failure," where the last repetition you do is almost impossible. While pushing until the muscles ache contributes to strength, don't push on if you're feeling real pain in the joints or elsewhere.

Stunt professionals keep their bodies well toned with a variety of exercises, from lifting weights to climbing rope.

Exercises such as chin-ups, pull-ups, and rope climbing can especially help because action performers must often hoist their own bodies. They may scramble up on a roof from a building ledge or shimmy up a rope to escape through a skylight. When no equipment is available, push-ups and sit-ups can keep the body toned.

FUELING THE BODY

Eating healthy is vital for the stunt performer. The better quality fuel you put in your body, the better it will perform. The diet for Thor's stunt double during training included lean proteins, like fish, turkey, boiled eggs, and chicken, healthy fats from foods like nuts and avocados, and complex carbohydrates, such as quinoa, sweet potatoes, and brown rice. Sometimes a role will require a stunt double to put on some muscle. Thor's double at one point ate thirty-five small meals a day and trained twice daily to try to approach the size of the actor Chris Hemsworth.

Stunt workers are super athletes and eat as such, often loading up on nutritious carbohydrates that supply immediate energy and proteins that contribute to muscle growth. Those who work out intensively can't forget to drink plenty of water. A body functions best when it's well hydrated. Plus, consuming plenty of water flushes out impurities and makes a person look better.

BUCKLE UP

The first concern for any stunt person is how to maintain safety. No director wants an actor to suffer an injury. Darrin Prescott is one of Hollywood's biggest stunt performers, coordinating and performing stunts in movies like *Baby Driver* (2017), *Captain America* (2011), and the *John Wick* films. He admits there's always some danger in stunt work and that's what makes it exciting. But his biggest worry is always safety.

The Screen Actors Guild-American Federation of Television and Radio Artists, the labor union for actors, agrees that its number-one priority is performer safety. The organization offers an online safety training course for stunt coordinators and loads of advice on its website.

No film or television production wants its performers to get hurt. The reality, too, is that accidents can be costly

The film *Baby Driver* features many nail-biting car chases, which are all well rehearsed and carefully planned to assure that no one gets hurt.

in both delaying filming and possible lawsuits. That's why all big projects have insurance to cover such unforeseen events, and productions companies do everything humanly possible to prevent accidents. The risks of every stunt have to be discussed in great detail with everyone on set. With careful planning, potential dangers can be reduced.

STUNTS GONE WILD!

While most stunts may dazzle and get audience hearts racing, some are certainly more outrageous than others. Here are a few of the craziest stunts that have been captured in film.

In the James Bond movie *Live and Let Die* (1973), the double for Roger Moore ran across the backs of several live crocodiles to make an escape. On the fourth take, one of the reptiles bit his foot.

Stuntman Dar Robinson holds the record for the highest wireless free-fall from a building in a commercial film. He took the 220-foot (67-meter) plunge out a window at the Hyatt Regency in Atlanta in the Burt Reynolds movie *Sharkey's Machine* (1981).

Actor and daredevil Jackie Chan performed the truly death-defying stunt of sliding down twenty-one stories of glass window panes, reportedly with no harness, padding, or net in the movie *Who Am I?* (1998).

In the Batman movie *The Dark Knight* (2008), a stuntman sent a huge eighteen-wheel truck flipping upside down on a Chicago street. A remote-controlled piston attached under the truck catapulted the vehicle. Director Christopher Nolan had seven cameras rolling because a stunt like this is not repeatable. Luckily, it all went off without a hitch.

The movie *Mad Max: Fury Road* (2015) featured some crazy high-speed stunts. The most memorable may be stuntmen who were attached to the top of 40-foot (12 m) high flexible poles connected to superfast vehicles. The performers learned to send themselves arching into other speeding vehicles and snatch those inside.

FAKING IT

Movies are all about creating illusions. When the stunt performer crashes through a brick wall, most likely that wall is not made of brick. Prop builders make bricks of Styrofoam and other light materials that will decrease injuries. The same idea goes into fake glass. Sugar glass, sometimes called candy glass or breakaway glass, lets actors smash through windows without cutting themselves or having shards embedded in their flesh. The same material is used to make fake bottles when it comes time to smash someone over the head with one.

BREAKING THE FALLS

High falls are one of the mainstays of action films. Descender rigs with wires that connect to harnesses are workhorses in the industry. When hooked up to one, the stunt performer is safeguarded from a devastating impact. Giant airbags and nets cushion dives taken from great heights, but still performers have to pay close attention to the setup. A few stunt performers have suffered serious injuries, and even death, when they did not land correctly on airbags or the airbags did not provide enough cushioning.

DRIVING LIKE MAD

Car chases and stunts continue to be a staple of the film and television business. Look at the success of the *Fast and Furious* franchise. There are currently ten *Fast and Furious* movies. Roll cages, helmets, fire extinguishers, and vehicle modifications help keep stunt drivers safe.

The roll cage is a special tubular frame that expert prop engineers build into vehicles to give them extra stability and strength. Heavy reinforcement allows cars to take

In the *Fast and the Furious* movies, the cars are specially built with roll cages. Stunt drivers train long and hard to safely handle these super-charged automobiles.

powerful hits and keep the driver safe. Stunt drivers secure themselves with safety belts and shoulder harnesses. The high-speed chase, rolls, jumps, and crashes on screen are executed by drivers with lots of experience. David Alessi, who has done high-speed driving for movies such as *Need for Speed* (2014) and *Ant-Man* (2015), developed his auto skills while working as a police officer and police driving instructor. Cost is also a factor in making sure a car stunt goes right—think how expensive it is to destroy a car on screen.

CHAPTER FOUR

THE UNSUNG HEROES

Stunt performers have been called the unsung heroes of film and television because they make exciting action scenes possible, yet their names fly by in the credits. The movie stars get all the attention and high salaries, but very few audience members know who the stunt performers are. The Screen Actors Guild gives annual awards for stunt ensemble work, but the Academy Awards still doesn't give an Oscar for stunt work.

Many stunt performers know that their work can be a big reason why a movie is successful and think they deserve more recognition. Others are less concerned with getting attention. In an interview in *Entertainment Weekly*, Jonathan Eusebio, the stunt coordinator on *Black Panther* (2018), said, "We're behind-the-scenes guys and we just want to be part of a good movie."

Without Eusebio's talents, *Black Panther* would probably not be the blockbuster hit it became. Darrin Prescott also worked as a stunt coordinator on *Black Panther*, as well as on hit films such as *Spider-Man*, *Baby Driver*, *John Wick (2014)*, and *The Hangover (2009)*. Prescott says he got his drive for thrill seeking as a boy, riding bikes and motorcycles, and trying jumps off of ramps. When he became an adult, he knew he had to move to Hollywood and try stunt work.

CAITLIN DECHELLE

For Caitlin Dechelle, her path to becoming a stunt double in *Wonder Woman* and other movies began at age six when she began studying martial arts. Along the way, she earned three black belts—in Chinese kenpo, Japanese goju-ryu, and taekwondo. In college, she studied to be an orthodontist. But she really wanted more exciting, physical work. Her pursuit of stunt work clearly has paid off.

Like many stunt people, Caitlin Dechelle began building her physical skills as a youngster. Her study of martial arts paid off when she began her career.

JANESHIA ADAMS-GINYARD

Janeshia Adams-Ginyard began her journey to stunt work as a young girl dedicated to athletic excellence. In high school, she was a star athlete in track and volleyball. Her high school selected her as athlete of the year. She also learned to wrestle and do taekwondo. When she saw an actor running in a movie, she thought she could do that and do it better than what she was seeing. She has gone on to appear in *Black Panther* and *Avengers: Infinity War* (2018).

Adams-Ginyard recognizes that there still aren't too many African American women in the stunt business but she hopes to pave the way for others and wants to inspire others to follow their dreams. In an interview on the website Black Girl Nerds, she said, "I want to make sure that I am a walking inspiration, a walking testimony to somebody to be like, 'No, I can't stop, I gotta keep going, because if I stop, I do know that tomorrow won't be better.'"

Janeshia Adams-Ginyard, who was a high school athlete, delivered action-packed sequences in the movie *Black Panther*. She hopes to inspire other young African American women who want to do stunt work.

STEVEN HO

In high school, Steven Ho competed in karate tournaments. Shortly after graduating, Ho was spotted by the Chinese

BREAKING INTO THE BIZ: NETWORKING IS KEY

Elisabeth Carpenter was very athletic from a young age. She loved to swing on, jump off, and climb on anything she could. At age seven, she began competing in gymnastics and stuck with it. At age thirteen, she auditioned for the international youth circus called Circus Smirkus. The circus hired her for four summers. As a young adult, she develop a career as an aerialist, acrobat, and contortionist, working for shows such as Cirque du Soleil, Cirque Mechanics, Dream World Cirque, and Eye of Newt Circus, to name a few.

Elisabeth Carpenter got into the stunt world by working hard and networking.

Her first film role was performing as an acrobatic elf in the movie *Polar Express* (2004), but she waited nine years after that to transition into full-time stunt work. In an interview with the author, she says she got into the field by having friends in stunt work who encouraged her. "We get all our jobs ourselves by networking, and meeting people at different gyms and training centers," she says. Carpenter recommends that young people interested in the field look into training facilities that specialize in teaching stunt work. They are not only good for developing skills but also for making job connections. "Half the battle is meeting people who work in the industry and learning from them," she says. "They see what your skill set is and they may know someone who will hire you."

Carpenter has now doubled for the lead actress, Shailene Woodley, in the *Divergent* movie series, *Captain Marvel* (2019), and for the fictional superheroine the Wasp. She also appears in *Avengers: Endgame* (2019). She tells students that the more skills they develop, the more work they will get. Carpenter studied

taekwondo, is scuba certified, and she has a motorcycle license. "The fun part has been learning things that I didn't know," she says. Her experience in movies has taught her about intensive fight choreography and the hours of rehearsal required to make an elaborate fight scene look effortless. Besides getting some type of athletic training, Carpenter advises students to do their homework: "Watch action films and read up on who were the greats in the business and who are working in big movies now and what their training is."

actor and martial artist Jet Li and recruited into stunt work. He popularized flashy jump kicks called the 540 and the Hawkeye. His martial arts talents landed him roles in the *Teenage Mutant Ninja Turtles* (1990) and *Pirates of the Caribbean* movies and *The Walking Dead*.

TJ STORM

TJ Storm is one of the biggest stars in motion pictures. After all, he is the actor who portrayed the 400-foot (122 m) tall Godzilla in the 2014 movie of the same name. He's also played the huge Colossus in the movie *Deadpool* (2016). He was also one of Hollywood's smallest stars, having acted as the 10-inch-tall (25-centimeter) Baby Groot from the film *Guardians of the Galaxy* (2014).

Through motion capture technology, Storm has played roles of all shapes and sizes, including many video game characters. In one day of video game work, he acted as twenty different characters. To do so, Storm wears a tight suit with little reflective markers all over it. Special cameras transfer his motions to a digital character that can be manipulated in a computer.

Playing so many characters requires imagination and Storm believes his "geeky" interests as a kid have helped him succeed. "Geekdom can turn into gold," he said in an interview with the author. "I played Dungeons and Dragons every day that I had a chance, and that serves me today because D&D is all about imagination." Storm also credits his mother for setting him on course for a stunt career by enrolling him in karate class at age seven. "My mom would not let me quit even though I wanted to," he says.

In high school, Storm pursued dancing to overcome his shyness. Break dancing was a way to fit in, and his talent won him more than two hundred dance contests. As a young adult, he kept up his training in martial arts and danced in music videos. The work just barely paid for rent and food, though.

Because of his martial arts skills (he is a three-time Martial Art Masters Hall of Fame inductee), Storm auditioned for kickboxing movies, and his career in stunt performance took off. In an interview with the author, he said: "Because I danced and choreographed and trained in the martial arts, I knew how to do fighting techniques well and relatively safely. Fighting and movement are still my specialties today."

He advises students to learn from mistakes and to think why certain actions work and others fail. He encourages young people to watch action films with a critical eye. "By studying films, I added different

TJ Storm often lands roles that are suited to his athletic ability. With motion capture technology, Storm has played many roles, from the giant Godzilla to the tiny Baby Groot.

moves to my repertoire," he says. "If you want to be in this business, you'll have a huge advantage if you love watching movies and being physical and love to perform. If you've watched a lot of action films, you have a much larger vocabulary and knowledge base to draw from as a professional."

One of the biggest things that those new to the field need to learn is teamwork, according to Storm. "Stunt work is a team effort," he says. "Your team is going to patch you up, look out for dangers for you, and figure out how to make you look good. Nobody likes the lone wolf on a set. You have to know how to communicate with people, how to take direction, and how to be of service. You need to be part of a well-oiled unit."

In addition to performing, Storm runs an action acting school called Mind's Eye Tribe. He encourages students to get team experience by working on group projects or joining in a team sport. "I played on the basketball team, and it took me a while to realize it but the team worked because we all worked together." Teamwork is what being a stunt performer is all about.

GLOSSARY

aerialist An entertainer who performs high in the air on a tightrope, silks, or trapeze.

airbag A cushion that protects stunt workers during a fall.

air ram A pneumatic machine that catapults a performer through the air.

calisthenics A type of exercise performed without the assistance of equipment.

contortionist A performer who bends and twists his or her body into strange positions.

descenders Devices that lower actors by wires.

freerunning A type of "urban acrobatics" in which athletes run through obstacles with elaborate motions.

motion capture A process of digitally recording motion and then transferring those motions to a computer-animated character.

paraphernalia Miscellaneous items or equipment.

parkour An activity or sport that involves moving rapidly through an obstacle course.

polyurethane A type of plastic.

repertoire The collection of one's talents or skills.

roll cage A framework that reinforces a stunt car cabin.

squibs Miniature explosives used to simulate the impact of gunshots.

sugar glass A transparent form of sugar used to mimic glass.

taekwondo A modern Korean martial art form.

winch A lifting device using a rotating drum and rope, cable, or wire.

FOR MORE INFORMATION

Canadian Stuntmen's Association
8582 171 Street
Surrey, BC V4N 5J1
Canada
(888) 993-4566
Website: https://www.csastunts.com
Facebook: @CSAstunts
This group upholds high professional standards to ensure the high-quality production of Hollywood-level stunts.

International Stunt Association
4454 Van Nuys Boulevard, # 214
Sherman Oaks, CA 91403
(818) 501-5225
Website: http://www.isastunts.com
Facebook: @internationalstuntschool
Instagram and Twitter: @ISAstunts
International Stunt Association is an organization for stunt work professionals that provides news, career connections, and skill development.

Screen Actors Guild-American Federation of Television and Radio Artists (SAG-AFTRA)
5757 Wilshire Boulevard
Los Angeles, CA 90036
(855) 724-2387
Website: http://www.sagaftra.org
Facebook: @SAGAFTRA
Instagram and Twitter: @sagaftra
This labor union represents television and film actors and offers industry resources and news.

Stuntmen's Association
200 Lankershim Bouelvard, #190
North Hollywood, CA 91601
(818) 766-4334
Website: http://www.stuntmen.com
Facebook: @sampstuntmen
Instagram and Twitter: @SampStuntmen
Stuntmen's Association is an organized group of stunt coordinators and stuntmen that offers support and materials for professionals in the industry.

Union of British Columbia Performers/Alliance of Canadian Cinema, Television and Radio Artists (UBCP/ACTRA)
380 W 2nd Avenue
Vancouver BC V5Y 1C8
Canada
(604) 689-0727
Website: http://www.ubcp.com
Facebook: @UBCP.ACTRA
Instagram and Twitter: @UBCP_ACTRA
UBCP/ACTRA is a Canadian trade union for performers that provides a special web page of services and resources for stunt workers.

United Stuntwomen's Association
26893 Bouquet Cyn Road
Suite C, Box #218
Saugus, CA 91350
Website: http://www.usastunts.com
This organization works to connect stuntwomen with job opportunities and promote professional standards.

FOR FURTHER READING

Bauer, Laura. *Hollywood Heroines: The Most Influential Women in Film History*. Greenport, CT: Greenwood Publishing, 2018.

Burgio, Danielle. *The Stuntwoman's Workout: Get Your Body Ready for Anything*. San Francisco, CA: Chronicle Books, 2005.

Ciarfalio, Carl. *Stars, Stunts and Stories: A Hollywood Stuntman's Fall to Fame.* Whiting, IA: Ryan Publishing, 2015.

Freese, Gene. *Classic Movie Fight Scenes*. Jefferson, NC: McFarland Publishing, 2017.

Gordon, Nick. *Dangerous Jobs: Stunt Performer*. New York, NY: Scholastic, 2013.

Gregory, Molly. *Stuntwomen: The Untold Hollywood Story*. Lexington, KY: University Press of Kentucky, 2018.

Lane, Andrew. *Movie Stunts & Special Effects: A Comprehensive Guide to Planning and Execution.* London, England: Bloomsbury Academic, 2014.

McCollum, Sean. *The World's Most Daring Stunts*. Mankato, MN: Capstone Publishing, 2016.

Needham, Hal. *Stuntman! My Car-Crashing, Plane-Jumping, Bone-Breaking, Death-Defying Hollywood Life*. New York, NY: Little, Brown and Company, 2011.

Smith, Dean. *Cowboy Stuntman: From Olympic Gold to the Silver Screen*. Lubbock, TX: Texas Tech University Press, 2013.

BIBLIOGRAPHY

Armstrong, Vic. *The Adventures of the World's Greatest Stuntman: My Life as Indiana Jones, James Bond, Superman, and Other Movie Heroes*. London, England: Titan Publishing Group, 2011.

Associated Press. "5 filming accidents that rocked, helped shape the industry." AP, November 20, 2016. https://apnews.com.

Avery, Jim. "5 Movie Stunts That Looked Even Crazier Behind The Scenes." Cracked, January 26, 2018. http://www.cracked.com/article_25258_5-movie-stunts-that-looked-even-crazier-behind-scenes.html.

Barnes, Katie. "Stunt double Caitlin Dechelle on 'Wonder Woman' and her real-life superpowers." ESPN, June 2, 2017 http://www.espn.com/espnw/culture/article/19510724/stunt-double-caitlin-dechelle-wonder-woman-real-life-superpowers.

Burgio, Danielle. *The Stuntwoman's Workout: Get Your Body Ready for Anything*. San Francisco, CA: Chronicle Books, 2005.

Carpenter, Elisabeth. Interview by Don Rauf. February 17, 2019.

Conley, Kevin. *The Full Burn*. New York, NY: Bloomsbury USA, 2008.

Furminger, Sabrina. "Anatomy of a stunt: How to set yourself on fire and survive." *Vancouver Courier*, October 23, 2013. https://www.vancourier.com.

Handel, Jonathan. "'Walking Dead' Stuntman Death: New Investigation Details Emerge." *Hollywood Reporter*, July 19, 2017. https://www.hollywoodreporter.com.

Hinds, Carolyn. "BGN Interview: Stuntwoman and Actress Janeshia Adams-Ginyard of 'Black Panther.'" Black Girl Nerds, February 17, 2018. https://blackgirlnerds.com/bgn-interview-janeshia-adams-ginyard.

Idelson, Karen. "For Real Action, There's No Substitute for Stunt Professionals in Movie Production." *Variety*, January 17, 2018. https://variety.com/2018/artisans/production/stunt-professionals-movies-1202665765.

King, Susan. "A Woman's Place Is in the Action Roles." *Los Angeles Times*, July 5, 1998. http://articles.latimes.com/1998/jul/05/entertainment/ca-782/2.

Logan, C. J. "Stunt Master." *Muscle & Performance*, February, 5, 2014. https://www.muscleandperformance.com/training-performance/stunt-master.

Mink, Casey. "Want to Do Your Own Stunts? Here's What You Need to Know." *Backstage*, August 20, 2018. https://www.backstage.com/magazine/article/want-stunts-need-know-130.

Nevins, Jake. "'It's a terribly fine line': the stunt performers risking their lives for Hollywood." *The Guardian*, August 18 2017. https://www.theguardian.com/film/2017/aug/18/film-stunt-performers-injuries-deaths-hollywood.

Renee, V. "Shooting Simple Stunts: Get Enough Coverage of an Actor Getting Hit in the Face by a Frisbee." No Film School, July 22, 2013. https://nofilmschool.com/2013/07/tutorial-shooting-simple-stunts.

Robinson, Melia. "Day in the Life: How Bobby Holland Hanton Stays in Shape as a Stunt Double for Chris Hemsworth and Daniel Craig." Business Insider, October 8, 2013. https://www.businessinsider.com/day-in-the-life-of-a-stunt-double-2013-9.

Romano, Nick. "What if the Oscars awarded stunts?" *Entertainment Weekly*, January 2, 2019. https://ew.com/movies/2019/01/02/best-movie-stunts-2018-oscars.

Rose, Jane. "16 Behind-the-Scenes Secrets of Stunt Performers." Mental Floss, August 4, 2016. http://mentalfloss.com/article/84184/16-behind-scenes-secrets-stunt-performers.

Storm, TJ. Interview by Don Rauf. February 18, 2019.

INDEX

L

M

N

O

P

R

S

T

V

W

ABOUT THE AUTHOR

Don Rauf is the author of numerous books, including *Schwinn: The Best Present Ever, American Inventions: Big Ideas That Changed Modern Life*, and *Lost America: Vanished Civilizations, Abandoned Towns, and Erstwhile Roadside Attractions*. He has interviewed such celebrities as Johnny Depp, astrophysicist Neal deGrasse Tyson, songwriter Tom Lehrer, fashion designer Liz Lange, and celebrity chef Marcus Samuelsson. He lives in Seattle, Washington. Rauf can't resist a good action film, but the closest he has gotten to stunt work is riding the Cyclone rollercoaster at Coney Island.

PHOTO CREDITS

Cover, p. 1 Sergey Lavrentev/Shutterstock.com; p. 5 Frederick Florin/AFP/Getty Images; p. 7 Ullstein Bild/Getty Images; pp. 8–9 Murray Close/Moviepix/Getty Images; p. 11 roller coaster/ Fairfax Media/Getty Images; p. 15 Dorling Kindersley/Getty Images; p. 16 Bobby Bank/WireImage/Getty Images; p. 19 Mark Mainz/Getty Images; p. 23 AdMedia/Newscom; p. 24 Peathegee Inc/Getty Images; pp. 26–27 Entertainment Pictures/Alamy Stock Photo; p. 30 Ollie Millington/Getty Images; p. 32 Tara Ziemba/ Getty Images; p. 33 Jean Baptiste Lacroix/WireImage/Getty Images; p. 34 Macushla Wells; pp. 36–37 Used with permission; cover and interior graphic elements AdrianHillman/iStock/Getty Images (base jumper silhouette), RDC_design/iStock/Getty Images (orange grunge background), Vijay Patel/DigitalVision Vectors/Getty Images (black dots background).

Design and Layout: Michael Moy; Photo Researcher: Sherri Jackson